How Old Ar...

Cut out the candles below. Paste some on the cake to show how old you are.

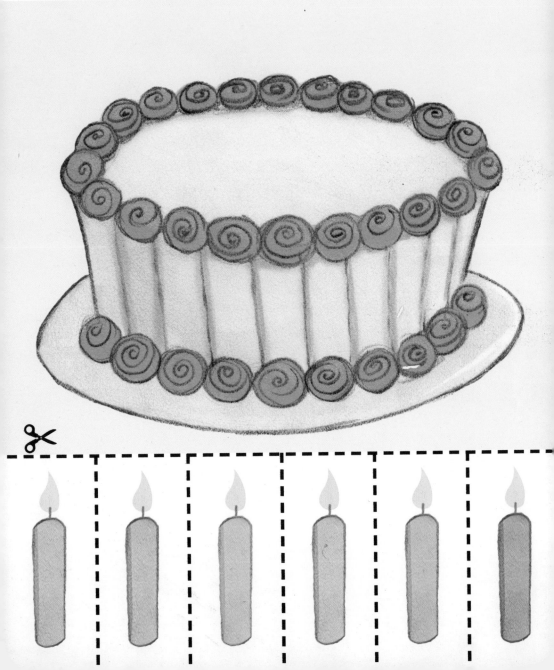

Counting Sheep

Cut out the numbers at the bottom of the page. Then paste each to fill in the missing numbers from 1 to 12.

Counting Campout

Connect the dots from **1** to **12** to see something you take camping.

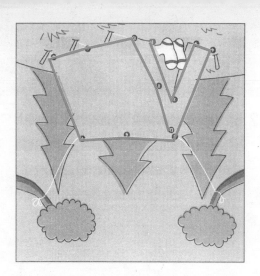

A Trip to the Park

These pictures are mixed up! Draw a circle around what you think happened **first**. Draw a line under what you think happened **last**.

Look at the color of the sky to figure out what happened first!

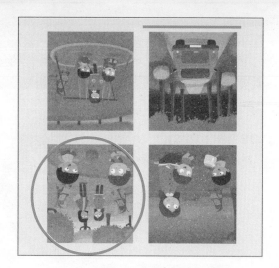

0 zero

This is the number 0.
This is the word zero.
This is one way to show 0. ⬜⬜⬜⬜⬜⬜

Trace the number 0. Then write your own.

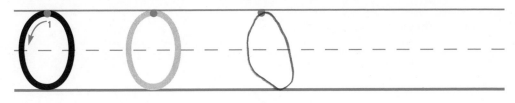

Trace the word zero. Then write your own.

Follow the 0's to help Arty bring a raisin to the picnic.

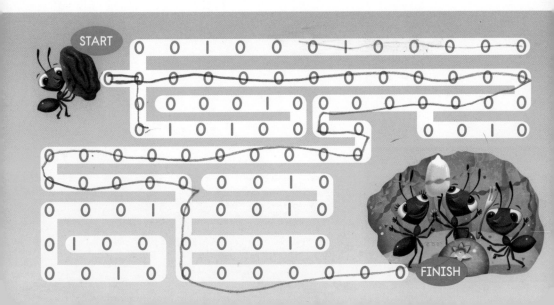

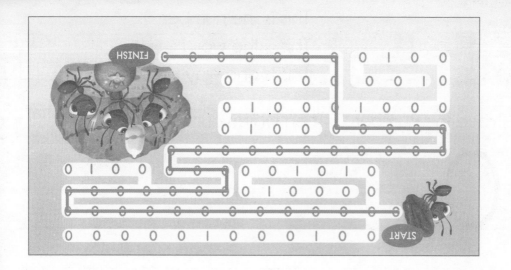

Boxed In

Circle the juice boxes that have **0** straws. Then draw a line between the **2** juice boxes that are an exact match.

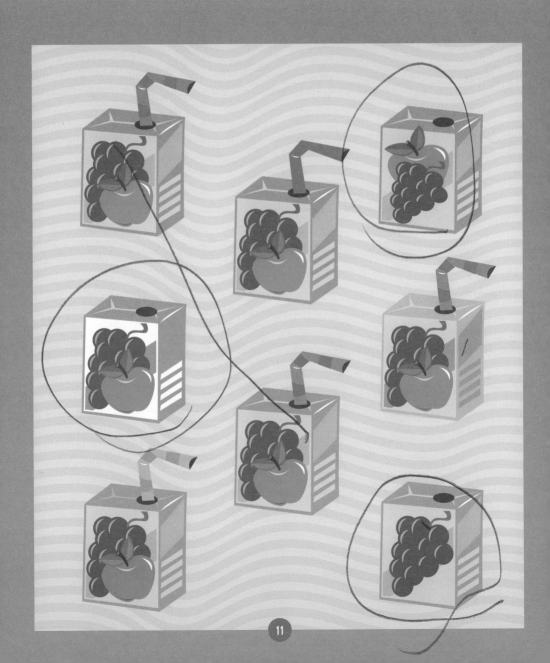

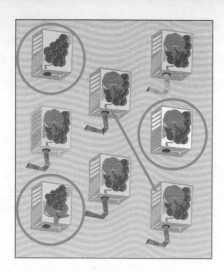

1 one

This is the number 1.
This is the word one.
This is one way to show 1.

Trace the number 1. Then write your own.

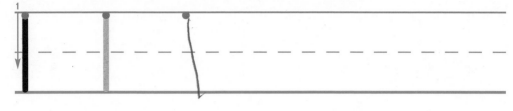

Trace the word one. Then write your own.

Circle the hat with 1 flower on it. Then follow each path to see which hat each hedgehog will wear.

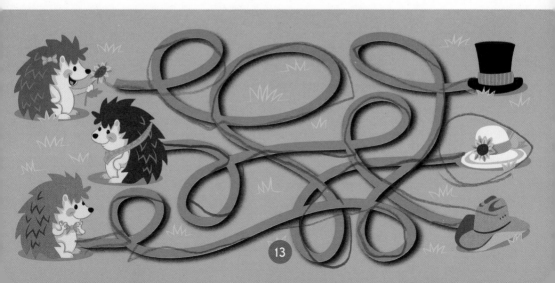

13

One Summer Day

Find and count: 1 sailboat ⛵, 1 dog 🐕, and 1 airplane ✈. What other groups of 1 can you find?

15

2 two

This is the number **2**.
This is the word **two**.
This is one way to show **2**.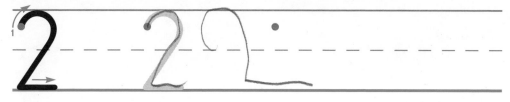

Trace the number **2**. Then write your own.

Trace the word **two**. Then write your own.

Circle the group with just **2** ladybugs.
Then draw a line between the
2 groups that match.

How many leaves are under each group of ladybugs?

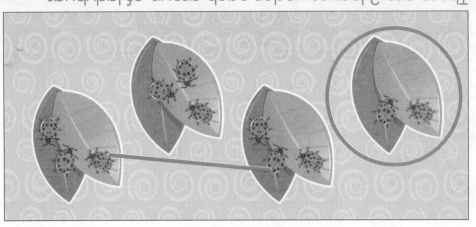

Double Fun

Circle the differences you see between these pictures.

Find and count **2** eggs in the top picture. What other groups of **2** do you see?

3 three

This is the number **3**.
This is the word **three**.
This is one way to show **3**. ⬛●●●⬜⬜

Trace the number **3**. Then write your own.

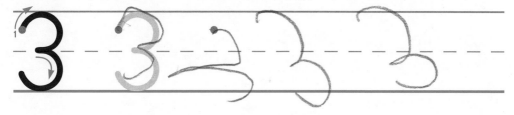

Trace the word **three**. Then write your own.

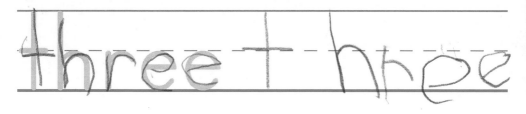

Count the **3** cows. Then follow the path with **3**'s to lead them to the barn.

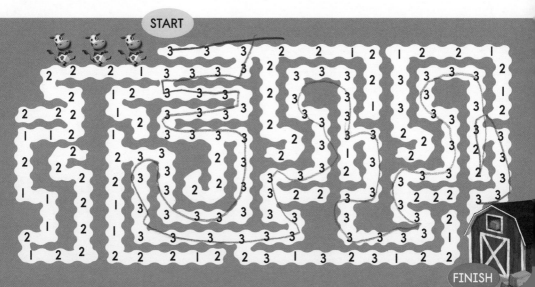

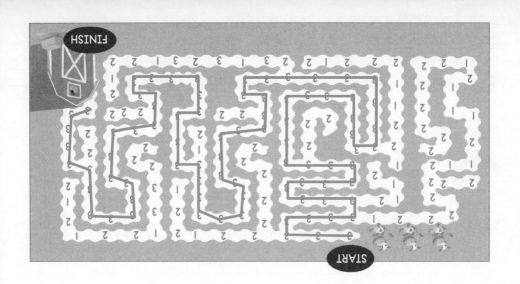

Go Fish!

Count the fish in each tank and write the number. Circle the tanks with **3** fish. Then draw a line from each tank to the tank with the same number of fish.

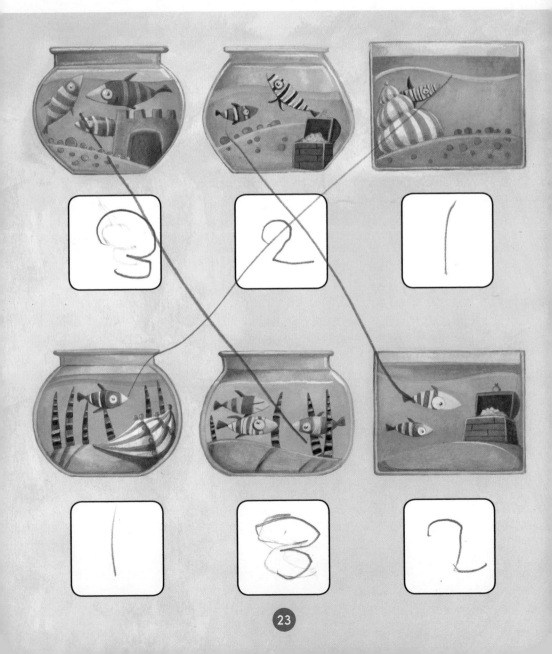

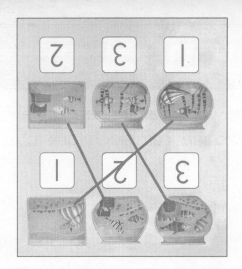

On Your Mark...

Can you find **1** frog, **2** blue cars, and **3** red flags?

Circle the numbers 1, 2, and 3 in the picture.

4 four

This is the number 4.
This is the word **four**.
This is one way to show 4. ⊡⊙⊙⊙⊙☐

Trace the number 4. Then write your own.

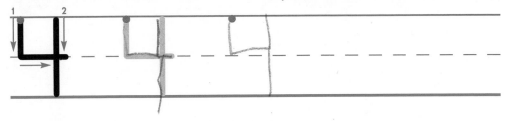

Trace the word **four**. Then write your own.

Count the trucks in each group. Then circle the group with 4 trucks.

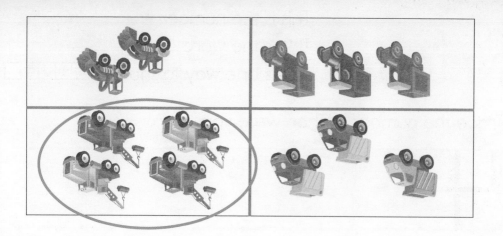

Fox Trot

Find and count 4 foxes, 4 pine trees, and 4 flowers.

Find and circle the 4 objects in this Hidden Pictures puzzle.

glove   spoon   tennis ball   cup

5 five

This is the number **5**.
This is the word **five**.
This is one way to show **5**.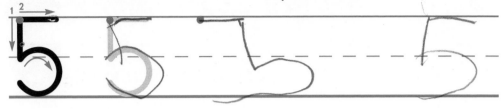

Trace the number **5**. Then write your own.

Trace the word **five**. Then write your own.

Count the **5** frogs. Then try to say the tongue twister **5** times.

Five fun-loving frogs

The Big Race

Find and count **5** runners and **5** prizes. What other things in groups of **5** do you see?

Follow each path to see what place each runner comes in.

6 six

This is the number **6**.
This is the word **six**.
This is one way to show **6**.

Trace the number **6**. Then write your own.

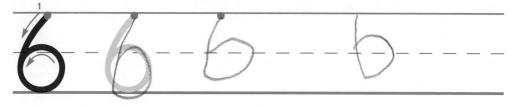

Trace the word **six**. Then write your own.

Circle the dog who's dreaming of **6** bones.

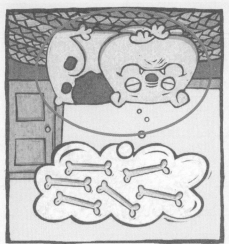

Game Day

Find and count **6** baseball caps.

Find and circle the **6** objects in this Hidden Pictures puzzle.

boot

hammer

horseshoe

golf club

umbrella

glove

37

Perfect Pie

Can you find **4** penguins, **5** people, and **6** pigeons?
Cross off the objects as you count them.

What do these pies have in common?

pumpkin-pineapple

peach

plum

Pie-Baking Contest

All the pies start with the letter *P*.

7 seven

This is the number 7.
This is the word seven.
This is one way to show 7.

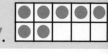

Trace the number 7. Then write your own.

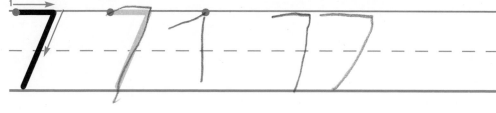

Trace the word seven. Then write your own.

Count the monsters in each group. Circle the group with 7.

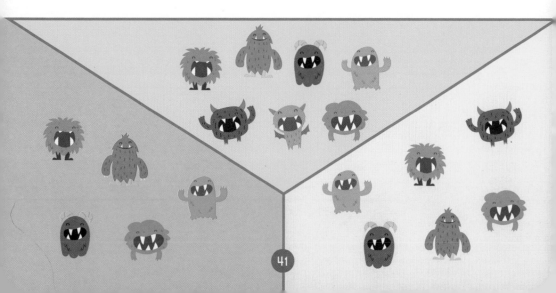

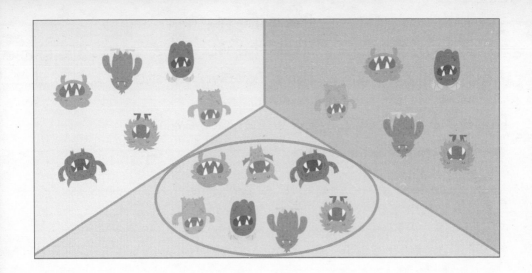

Let It Snow!

Count the **7** snowmen. Then draw a line between the 2 that are the same.

8 eight

This is the number 8.
This is the word eight.
This is one way to show 8.

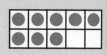

Trace the number 8. Then write your own.

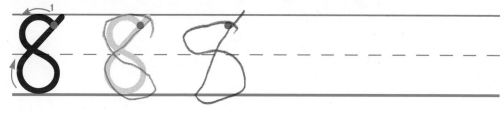

Trace the word **eight**. Then write your own.

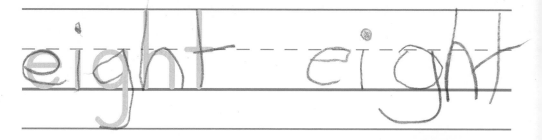

Count the plates in each stack.
Circle the stack with 8 plates.

Can you think of a word that rhymes with skate and plate?

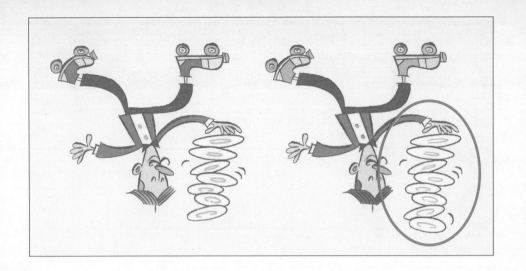

Cat Naps

Count the **8** cats. Then follow the **8**'s to help the mouse reach the cheese.

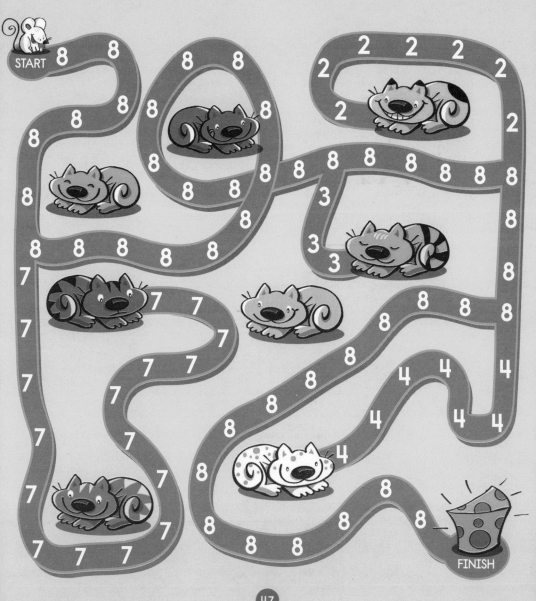

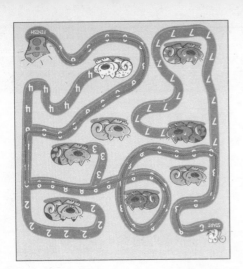

9 nine

This is the number 9.
This is the word **nine**.
This is one way to show 9.

Trace the number 9. Then write your own.

Trace the word **nine**. Then write your own.

nine

Color in each space with a 9 to see a sweet treat.

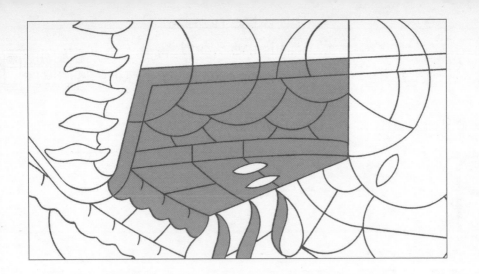

Pajama Party

Count 9 llamas at the sleepover. Then find and circle at least 9 differences between these pictures.

Summer Show

Can you find **7** dogs, **8** people wearing a hat or headband, and **9** bags of popcorn? Cross them off as you count.

10 ten

This is the number 10.
This is the word zero.
This is one way to show 10.

Trace the number 10. Then write your own.

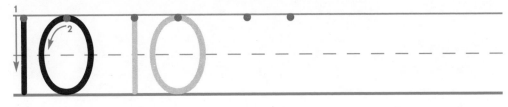

Trace the word **ten**. Then write your own.

ten

Count the stars on the balloons. Circle the balloon with 10 stars.

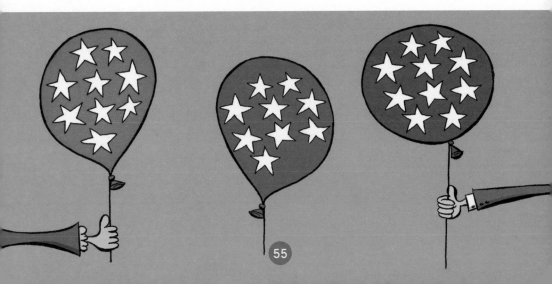

Time to Race

Find and count 10 mice.

Find and circle the 10 objects in this Hidden Pictures puzzle.

heart

envelope

watermelon

ring

candle

snake

candy cane

spoon

scissors

ruler

11 eleven

This is the number 11.
This is the word **eleven**.
This is one way to show 11.

Trace the number 11. Then write your own.

Trace the word **eleven**.

eleven

Count the fish. Circle the shirt with 11 fish.

Up, Up, and Away!

Count the **11** balloons. Then draw a design on the biggest balloon.

12 twelve

This is the number 12.
This is the word twelve.
This is one way to show 12.

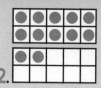

Trace the number 12. Then write your own.

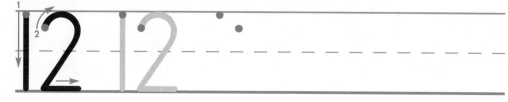

Trace the word twelve.

twelve

Count the 12 cupcakes. Then draw lines to match the cupcakes that are the same.

A dozen is a group of 12.

Frozen Fun

Count the 12 polar bears at the pond. How many animals are wearing hats?

12 animals are wearing hats.

Critter Count

Find and count **10** ladybugs, **11** butterflies, and **12** snails.

Counting Cars

In every row, count the vehicles in each of the **2** groups. Circle the groups if they are equal. Need a hint? Draw a line to pair up each object in the first group with an object in the second group. If every object is paired up, the groups are equal.

Equal means that groups have the same number.

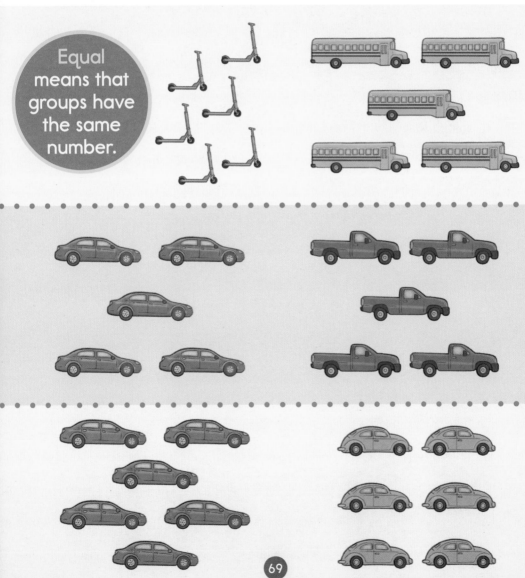

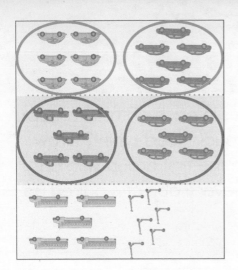

Who's Crabby?

Count the number of crabs. Then count the number of creatures in each group at the bottom of the page. Which group has the same, or **equal**, number as the crabs? Cut out that group and paste it next to the crabs.

These 2 groups are equal. They have the same number.

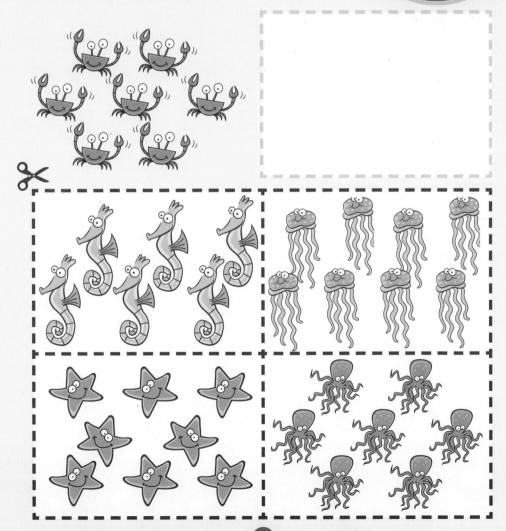

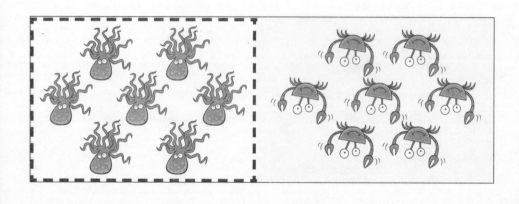

More Monsters

Count the monsters. In each row, circle the group that has more, or is **greater than**, the other group.

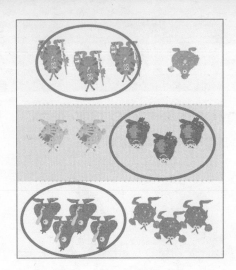

Go Fetch!

Count the number of dogs in each group. Which group has more dogs, or is **greater than**, the top group? Cut out that group and paste it next to the top section.

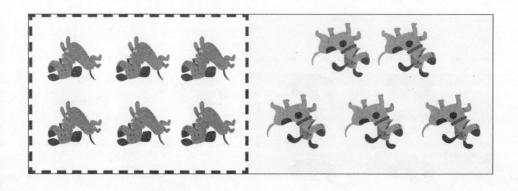

Less Lollipops

Count the lollipops. In each row, circle the group that has fewer, or is **less than**, the other group.

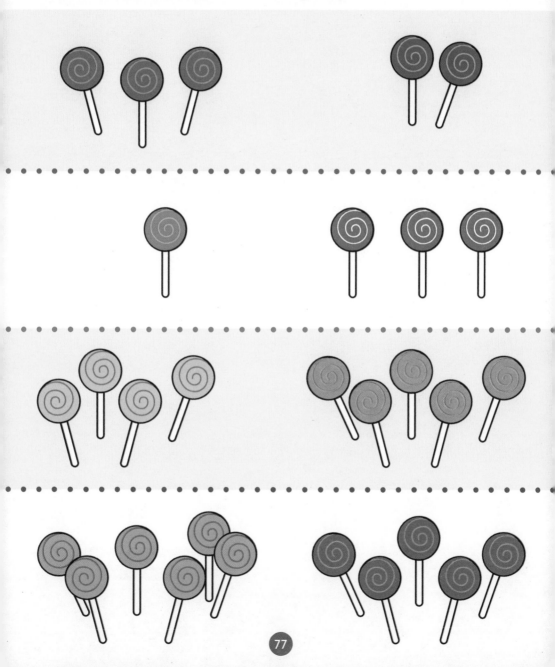

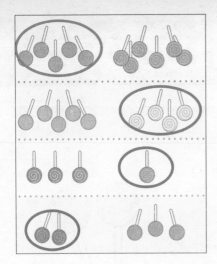

Feathered Friends

Count the number of birds in each group. Which group has fewer birds, or is **less than**, the top group? Cut out that group and paste it next to the top section.

Backyard Buddies

Greater than means a group has more objects. **Less than** means a group has fewer objects.

Count the birds in each group. Circle the **2** groups that are **equal**.

Count the squirrels in each group. Circle the group that is **greater than** the other group.

Count the rabbits in each group. Circle the group that is **less than** the other group.

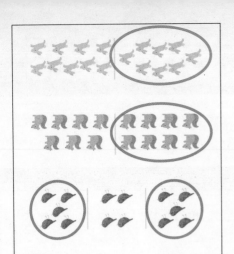

Dino-mite!

Greater than means a group has more objects. **Less than** means a group has fewer objects.

Circle the group that is **equal** to the first group.

Circle the group that is **greater than** the first group.

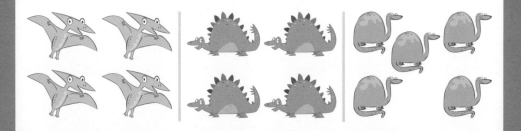

Circle the group that is **less than** the first group.

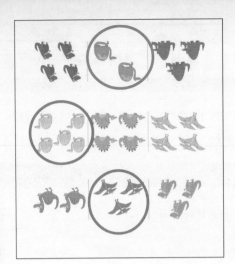

Big and Small

Cut out the animals at the bottom of the page. Paste the **big** animal next to the big elephant. Paste the **small** animal next to the small mouse.

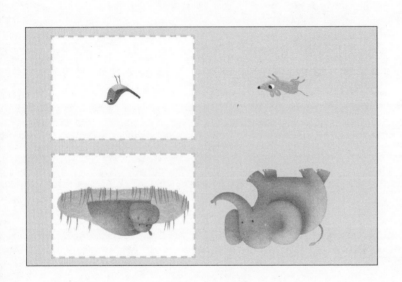

Tall and Short

Cut out the animals at the bottom of the page. Paste the **tall** animal next to the tall tree. Paste the **short** animal next to the short flower.

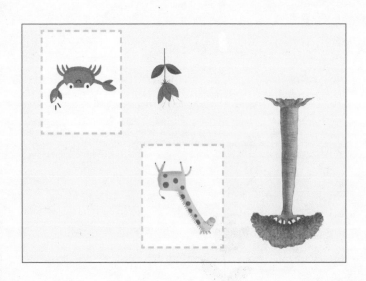

Long and Short

Cut out the saws at the bottom of the page. Paste the **long** saw next to the long screwdriver. Paste the **short** saw next to the short screwdriver.

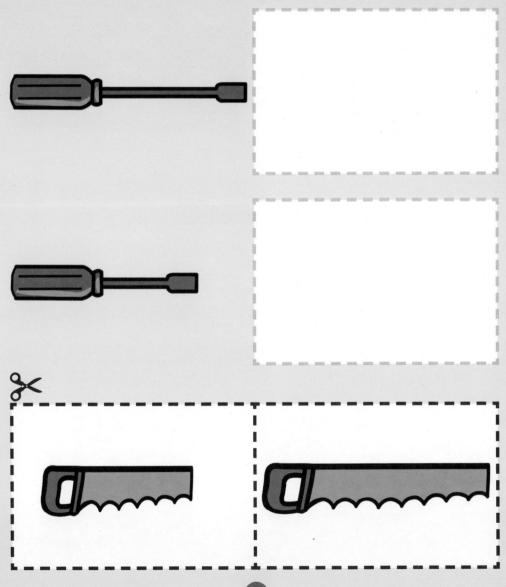

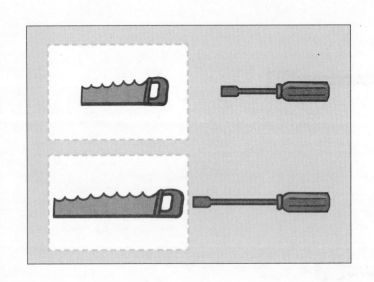

Big Birds

Cut out the **3** birds. Then paste them in size order from **big** to **biggest**.

big   bigger   biggest

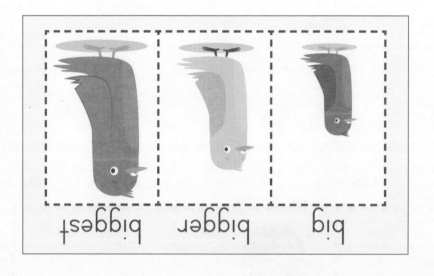

big bigger biggest

Small Talk

Circle the **smallest** snail.

Cut out the **3** birds. Then paste them in size order from **small** to **smallest**.

small	smaller	smallest

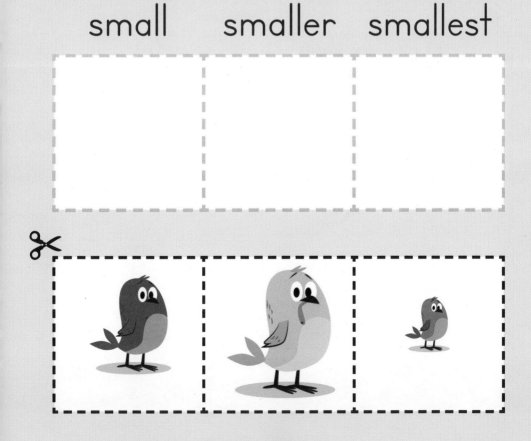

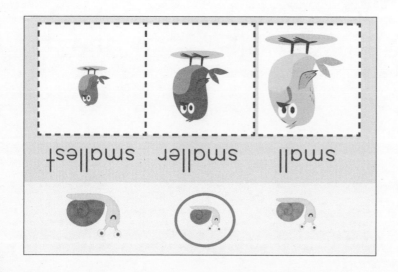

small   smaller   smallest

Snow Way!

Count the buttons on each snowman and write the number in the boxes. Draw a line between the **2** snowmen with the same number of buttons.

Draw a ○ around the snowman with the most buttons. Draw a ☐ around the snowman with the fewest buttons.

Full and Empty

Cut out the **full** glass, **full** sand pail, and **full** apple barrel. Paste each next to its **empty** version.

Heavy and Light

Cut out each **light** object. Then paste it next to the **heavy** item with the same color.

Something that is heavy weighs a lot. Something that is light does not weigh much.

Can you find light and heavy objects in your home?

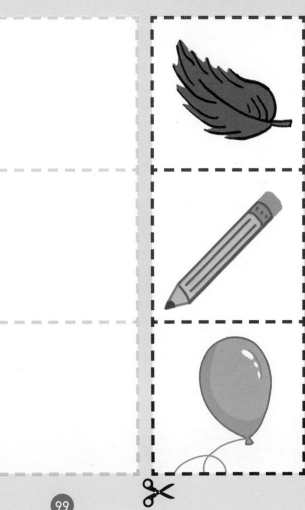

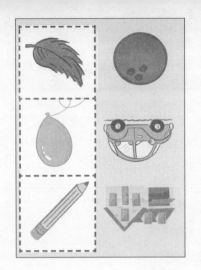

Circle

A **circle** is round. Trace the circle.
Then draw your own.

Cut out the **2** circles. Then paste them on the washing machines to complete the picture.

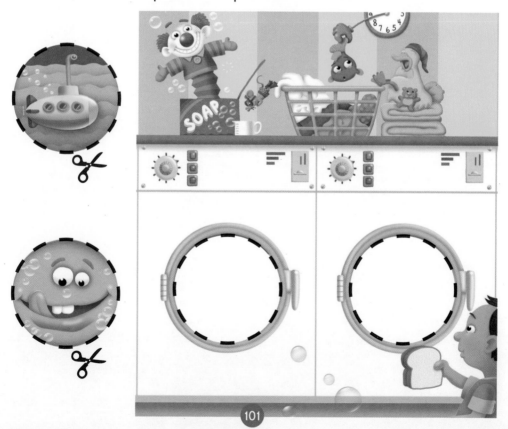

Square

A **square** has 4 sides that are the same length. Trace the square. Then draw your own.

Cut out the square at the bottom of the page. Paste it to complete the butterfly. Then draw and color in the wing to complete the butterfly.

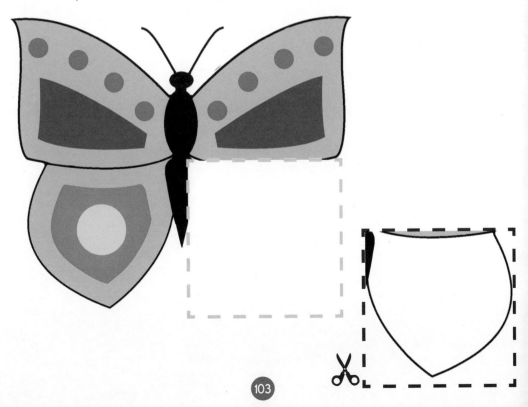

Triangle

A **triangle** has 3 sides. Trace the triangle. Then draw your own.

Cut out each slice of pizza at the bottom of the page. Then paste it below the slice that matches.

Rectangle

A **rectangle** has 2 long sides that are the same length and 2 short sides that are the same length. Trace the rectangle. Then draw your own.

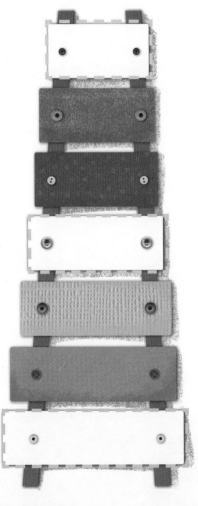

Cut out the **3** xylophone keys below. Then paste them into the correct places.

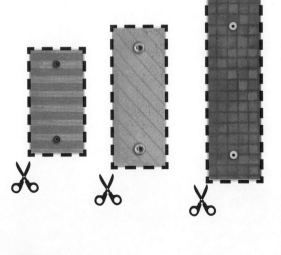

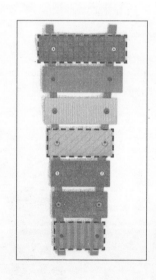

Rhombus

A **rhombus** is like a stretched square. Trace the rhombus. Then draw your own.

Trace the **2** rhombuses. Then find the **3** objects in this Hidden Pictures puzzle.

What other shapes do you see?

bowling ball

toothbrush

crescent moon

109

Oval

An **oval** is like a stretched circle. Trace the oval.
Then draw your own.

Find the **5** oval-shaped objects in this Hidden Pictures puzzle.

balloon

watermelon

egg

football

dish

111

Sphere

 A **sphere** is a solid, 3-D shape that is curved, like a ball.

This basketball is a sphere. Circle each sphere you see below.

Find and circle at least **10** differences between these pictures.

These are spheres.

Cube

A **cube** is a solid, 3-D shape with 6 equal faces, like this toy block.

Circle each cube you see below.

Cut out each toy block at the bottom of the page. Then paste them in number order below.

These are
cubes.

Pyramid

 A **pyramid** is a solid, 3-D shape with a flat base and 4 faces shaped like triangles.

Follow the pyramids to help Cal meet his friend!

START

FINISH

117

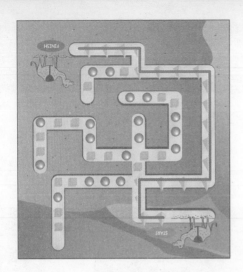

Shape Match-Up

Draw a line to match each solid, or 3-D, shape with its flat, or 2-D, match.

  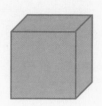

Draw lines between the matching beach balls. Circle the ball that does **not** have a match.

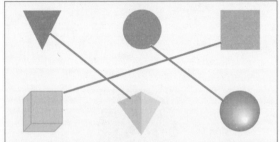

Shape Sorting

Cut out each shape below. Paste the circles in the circle area and the squares in the square area. Then count how many you pasted into each area and write the number.

circles

squares

How many circles?

How many squares?

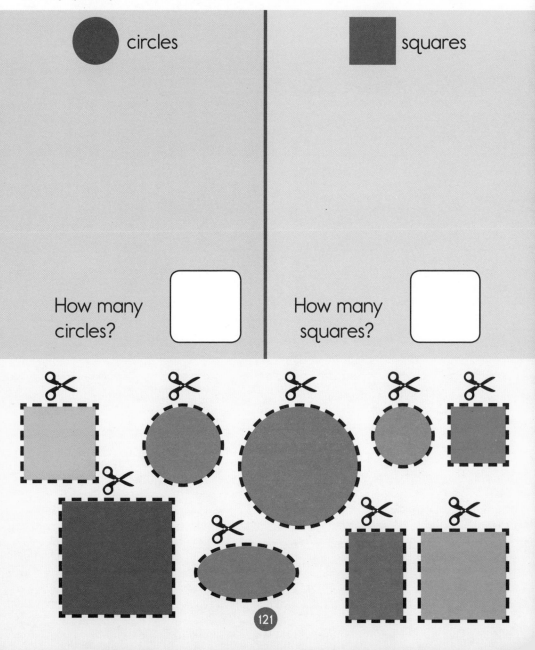

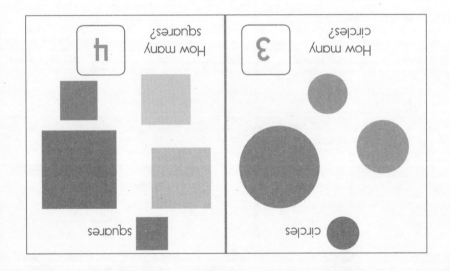

How many circles?

3

circles

How many squares?

4

squares

Color Sorting

Cut out each frog below. Paste it into the correct color area. Then count how many you pasted in each area and write the number.

yellow

blue

How many yellow frogs?

How many blue frogs?

Dots or Stripes?

Cut out each hot-air balloon below. Paste the ones with stripes in the stripes area and the ones with dots in the dots area. Then draw lines between the matching pairs.

Stripes	Dots

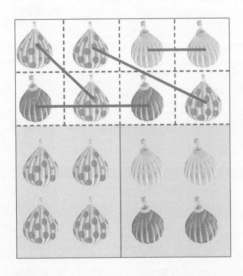

Go Sort

Cut out each vehicle below. Paste the boats in the boat area and the cars in the car area. Then count how many you pasted in each area and write the number.

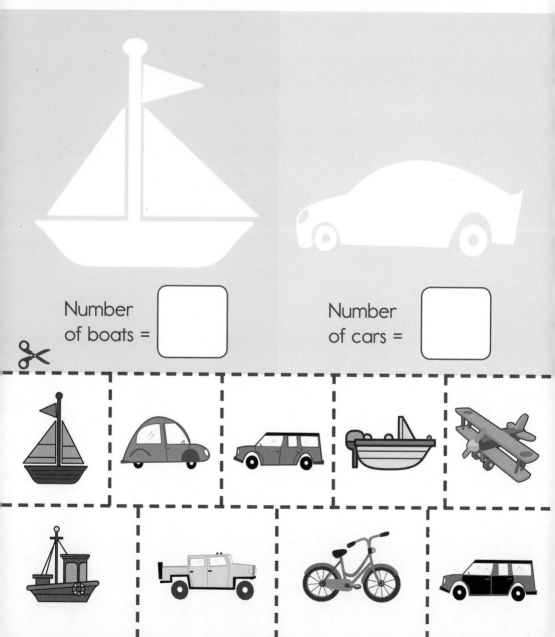

Number of boats =

Number of cars =

Number of boats = 3

Number of cars = 4

Tally Time

Count the number of each shape. Make that number of tally marks in the chart below.

Tally marks show how many.					
I	II	III	IIII	卌	卌 I
1	2	3	4	5	6

SHAPE	TALLY
▲	
■	
●	

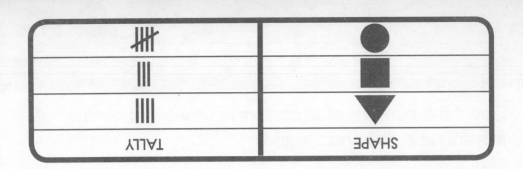

SHAPE	TALLY
▼	IIII
▮	III
●	IIII

Cut Flowers

Cut out each flower at the bottom of the page. Paste the flowers in the correct rows to complete the picture graph. Which group has the most flowers?

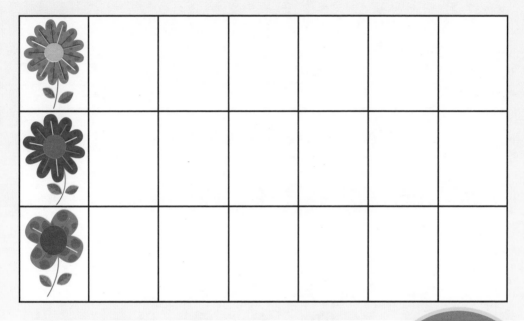

A picture graph shows how many there are of some objects.

The group of red flowers has the most.

Pet Count

Perry has **8** friends with pets. Cut out the pictures of their pets below. Then paste the dogs in the dog row, the cats in the cat row, and the fish in the fish row. Which group has the most pets?

Which pet would you like to have? Why?

The group of dogs has the most.

Kite Patterns

What kite comes next? Cut out the **6** kites at the bottom of the page. Paste them to finish the pattern in each row.

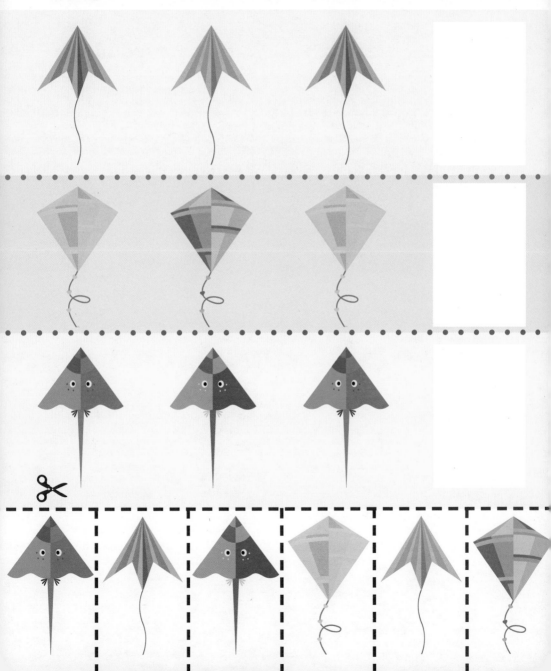

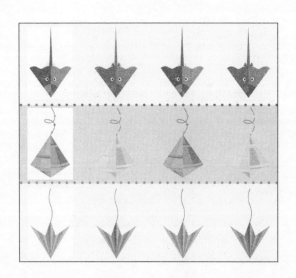

Shape Patterns

What shape comes next? Cut out the **6** shapes at the bottom of the page. Paste them to finish the pattern in each row.

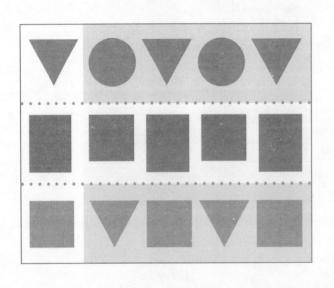

What Comes Next?

Cut out the **6** shapes at the bottom of the page. Paste them to finish the pattern in each row.

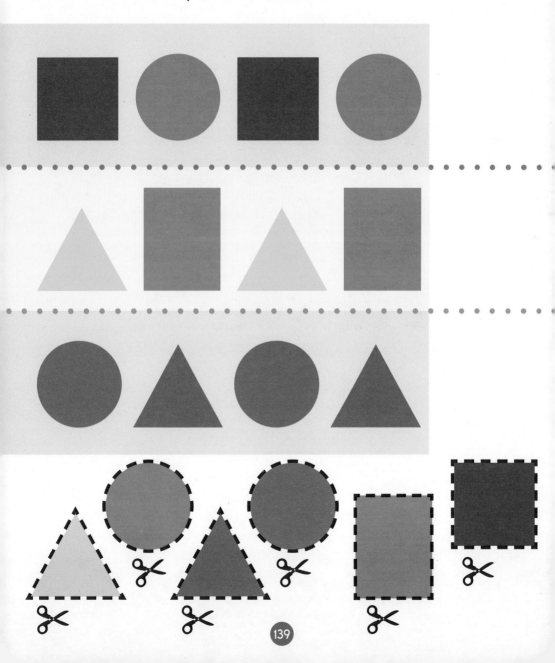

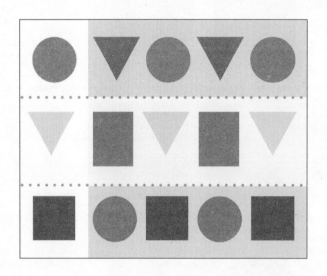

Space Path

Follow this pattern to help Zeep get to his spaceship.

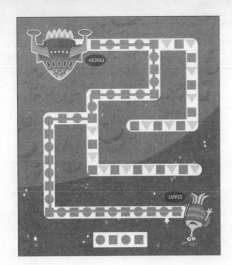

Silly Patterns

The red cans and blue cans make a pattern. What other patterns do you see?

What silly things do you see?

143

Farm Patterns

What comes next? Cut out the **6** pictures at the bottom of the page. Paste them to finish the patterns in each row.

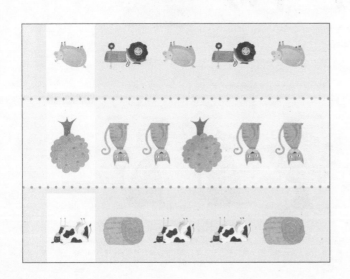

Make Patterns

Draw spots on the last ladybug to finish the pattern.

Add spots to these ladybugs to make a pattern.

Draw pepperoni slices on the last pizza to finish the pattern.

Add pepperoni slices to these pizzas to make a pattern.

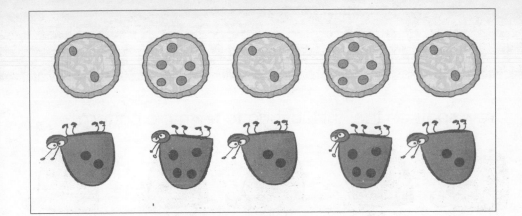

In Ben's Room

Help Ben find these items:

1. Draw a ◯ around the ball that is above the bed.
2. Put an ✗ on the hat that is on the bed.
3. Draw a ☐ around the toy that is in front of the dresser.

Point to a pattern in Ben's room.

Silly Store

What silly things do you see?

Cut out the **3** items from the bottom of the page. Paste the monkey **on top of** the purple bin. Paste the pumpkin **in front of** the purple bin. Paste the wagon **behind** the boy in the green jacket.

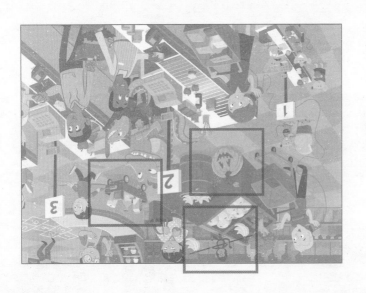

How Many Owls?

Cut out the **3** owls at the bottom of the page. Paste I owl in each row. Then count the number of owls in each row. Write the number in the box.

153

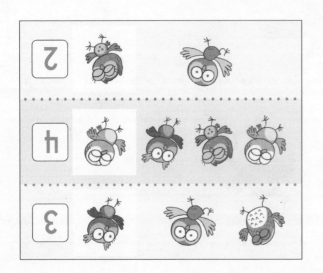

How Many Pigs?

Cut out the **6** pigs at the bottom of the page. Paste **2** pigs in each row. Then count the number of pigs in each row. Write the number in the box.

How Many Birds?

Count the birds in each row. Then write the number in the box.

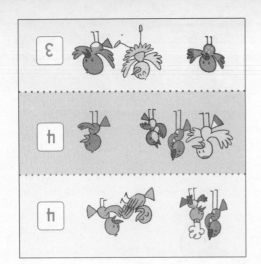

How Many Flamingos?

Count the flamingos in each row. Then write the number in the box.

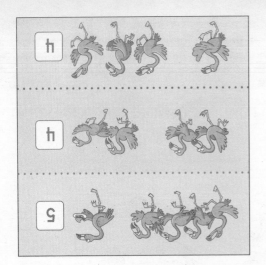

Make a 4

Count the crabs. Circle the 2 groups that make **4**.

Count the flowers. Circle the 2 groups that make **4**.

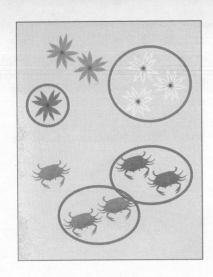

Make a 5

Count the ducks. Circle the 2 groups that make **5**.

Count the turtles. Circle the 2 groups that make **5**.

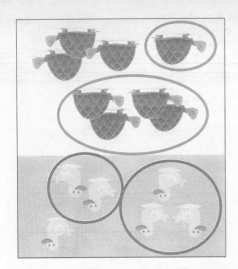

How Many Are Left?

Count the number of hedgehogs in this row. Cross off 1 hedgehog. How many are left (**0**, **1**, **2**, **3**, **4**, or **5**)? We did this one to get you started.

2

Count the hedgehogs. Cross off 1 hedgehog. How many are left?

Count the hedgehogs. Cross off 1 hedgehog. How many are left?

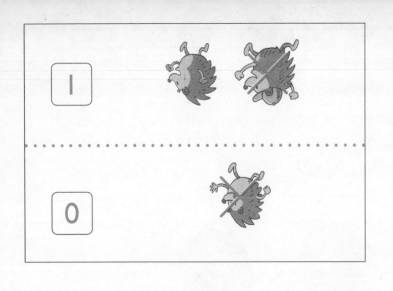

How Many Are Left?

Count the number of dogs in this row. Cross off **2** dogs. How many are left (**0**, **1**, **2**, **3**, **4**, or **5**)? We did this one to get you started.

Count the dogs. Cross off **2** dogs. How many are left?

Count the dogs. Cross off **2** dogs. How many are left?

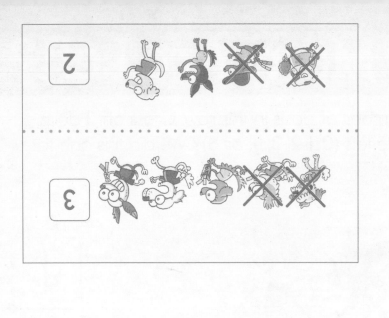

How Many Are Left?

Count the cows in this row. Cross off **1** cow. How many are left (**0**, **1**, **2**, **3**, **4**, or **5**)?

Count the cows. Cross off **2** cows. How many are left?

Count the cows. Cross off **3** cows. How many are left?

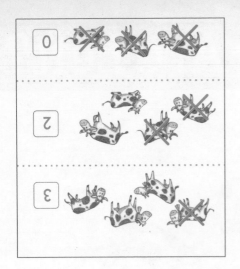

How Many Are Left?

Count the fish in this row. Cross off **3** fish. How many are left (**0, 1, 2, 3, 4,** or **5**)?

Count the fish. Cross off **2** fish. How many are left?

Count the fish. Cross off **1** fish. How many are left?

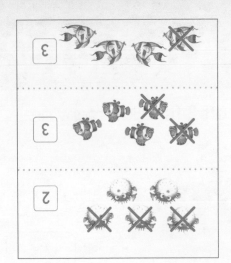

How Many?

Count the chickens in this row. How many do you need to cross off to make **3**? We did this one to get you started.

2

Count the chickens. How many do you need to cross off to make **2**?

Count the chickens. How many do you need to cross off to make **1**?

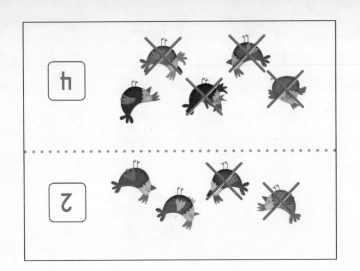

How Many?

Count the snowboarders in this row. How many do you need to cross off to make **4**? We did this one to get you started.

Count the snowboarders. How many do you need to cross off to make **3**?

Count the snowboarders. How many do you need to cross off to make **2**?

Investigate:
Air Power

Use the power of air to play hockey!

YOU NEED:

- a clean, empty pizza box • foil • straws • a large pompom
  - chenille stems or strips of cardboard • masking tape

1. Open the pizza box. Lay it on a flat surface.

2. Cover the inside of the box with foil.

3. Bend the chenille stems or cardboard strips to make goals.

4. Tape one goal to one end of the box. Tape the other goal to the other end.

5. The pompom is the hockey puck! Blow air through the straws to make it move. Try to get it through the other player's goal.

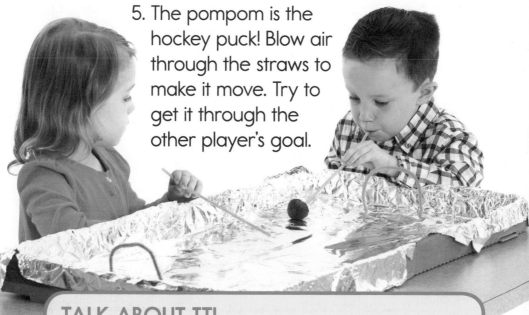

TALK ABOUT IT!

- How do you know that air is moving the pompom?
- Describe what happens when you blow softly into the straw and when you blow strongly.

Invent: Blowing in the Wind

A sailboat uses wind to move across water. Design a sailboat that you can move by blowing on it.

Wind is moving air. It has the power to move objects. What things might you see on a windy day?

YOU NEED:
• plastic lid   • craft foam shapes   • drinking straw
• play dough   • water in a sink or tub

1. Put some play dough on the inside of a plastic lid.
2. Ask an adult to make two holes along one side of a piece of craft foam with a hole punch or scissors. This is the sail.
3. Cut a straw in half. Put one half through the holes.
4. Stick the straw into the play dough.
5. Put your boat in water. Blow on the sail. What happens?
6. Improve your design. Try differently shaped foam sails. Change where you put the play dough.

TALK ABOUT IT!
• How did your boat sail? Which sail worked best? Did any other changes help it sail better? How did the boat sail when you blew air softly or strongly?
• What other things move when they are pushed by air?

Investigate:
What's in a Bean?

See what happens when beans grow!

YOU NEED:
- dried kidney beans • glass of water
- paper towel • zippered plastic bag

1. Put some beans in a glass of water. Let them soak for 3 hours.

2. Put the beans on a wet paper towel. Fold the towel over them.

3. Put the beans and the towel in the plastic bag.

4. Put the bag in a warm, dark place. Leave it there for 3 days.

5. Take out the beans. Split open one bean. What do you see?

TALK ABOUT IT!

- What happened to the beans?
- What did you see inside the bean you opened?
- What will happen to the beans if you plant them?

Investigate more: Grow Some Beans

YOU NEED:
- sprouted beans from page 179
- plastic cups
- potting soil

1. Put potting soil into the cups.
2. Put the seeds in the soil. Make sure the roots point down.
3. Put the cups in a sunny place.
4. Check the cups each day. Water the soil when it feels dry.

Draw to show how your beans grow.

A shoot pokes out of soil	A shoot grows leaves

TALK ABOUT IT!

- Why must you water the bean plants?
- Will bean plants grow without water?
- How can you test to find out?
- Will they grow without soil? What about without sunlight? How can you find out?

Roots grow down into the ground. Shoots grow up from the ground.

Investigate:
What a Puppy Needs

A puppy is a baby dog. Like all baby animals, it needs certain things to grow and be healthy. Circle the things that you think a puppy needs.

A puppy also needs lots of love. It needs people to make sure it is safe when it goes outside, too.

TALK ABOUT IT!

- How did you decide which things to circle?
- What do both puppies and human babies need to be healthy?
- What do puppies grow up to be? What other kinds of baby animals can you think of?

Invent: Design a Doghouse

Think about how your own home keeps you safe, dry, and warm. Young animals need shelter, too. Design a shelter, or home, for a puppy. Draw a picture of your design.

My Puppy Home

Share your design for a puppy home with an adult. Tell how it keeps the puppy safe, dry, and warm.

TALK ABOUT IT!

- Is your doghouse big enough for your growing puppy?
- Where would you put the doghouse? Why is that the best spot?

Investigate:
Touch and Feel

It's fun to find out how different objects feel. It's also fun to make a Touch and Feel collection!

YOU NEED:
- 8 pieces of paper • glue • objects with texture, such as feathers, sandpaper, bits of tree bark, cotton balls

1. Glue the objects to the pieces of paper. Put just one kind of object on each piece.
2. Let the glue dry.
3. Ask friends or family members to close their eyes and touch the objects one at a time. Have them guess what the objects are.

TALK ABOUT IT!

- Which objects are rough? Which objects are smooth? How do you know?
- What other words can you use to describe how the objects feel?
- Touch is one of our senses. What other senses do you use?

Investigate more:
Soft or Not?

Find objects in a box using just your sense of touch.

YOU NEED

- small objects, such as a spoon, a crayon, a key, plastic animals
- an empty tissue box

1. Put the objects in the box.
2. Ask a friend to feel inside the box to find an object you name. Take turns finding objects.

Your skin feels things because it has special sensors. These sensors send messages to your brain. Different sensors help you feel heat, pain, and more.

Circle the objects that would feel soft. Cross out the objects that would feel sharp or rough.

Investigate: Weather Watching

What's the weather like today? What was it like yesterday? Scientists record information about weather. You can, too!

YOU NEED:
- drawing paper
- crayons or markers

1. Draw a weather picture every day for one week.

2. At the end of the week, look at each picture you drew.

3. Count how many days were sunny. Count how many days were cloudy. Did it rain?

4. Try drawing a weather picture every day for a month!

Saturday, Sept. 1
Kylie
It is a sunny day.

Sunday, Sept. 2
Topa
It rained today.

TALK ABOUT IT!

- Was it mostly cloudy or mostly sunny all week? How do you know?

- When did the air feel cool or cold? When did it feel warm or hot?

- What else do you notice about the week's weather?

Investigate more:
Cloud Clues

Clouds can help you decide if you need an umbrella.

Look at these clouds. Circle the clouds that are a sign of a nice day. Cross out the clouds that mean rain is on the way.

Clouds are made of tiny water droplets or ice crystals.

Make a Cloud

You can make a cloud right in your home!

YOU NEED:
• a mirror

1. Put your mouth close to the mirror.
2. Breathe on the mirror. What happens?

TALK ABOUT IT!

How do you think the cloud on the mirror formed? (Remember that many clouds are made of water droplets.)

Investigate:
Fresh or Salt Water

What happens to sinking objects in salty water?

YOU NEED:
- 2 tall, clear glasses   • warm water   • ⅓ cup of salt
- blue food coloring   • 2 fresh eggs

1. Pour 1½ cups of warm water into each glass.

2. Add a drop of blue food coloring to one glass. This is your fresh water.

3. Add the salt to the other glass. Stir until the salt is mixed in.

4. Predict what will happen when you put eggs in both glasses.

5. Put one egg in fresh water. Put the other egg in salt water.

TALK ABOUT IT!

- What happened to the eggs? Were your predictions correct? Why or why not?

- Why do you think eggs might float in salt water but not in fresh water?

187

Investigate more:
Sink or Float?

What will sink and what will float in salty and fresh water? Experiment to find out!

YOU NEED:
- 2 tall, clear glasses
- warm water
- 1/3 cup of salt
- blue food coloring
- pairs of matching objects, such as balls of foil, small plastic toys, metal spoons

Salt water has lots of salt in it. The ocean is salty. Fresh water is not salty. Most rivers have fresh water.

1. Follow the directions on page 187 to make a glass of fresh water and a glass of salt water.
2. Predict what will happen when you put each pair of objects in both glasses.
3. Test each pair of objects. What happens?

TALK ABOUT IT!
- What did you find out?
- Did any objects sink in both fresh water and salt water? Why do you think they sank?
- What objects floated in both kinds of water? Why do you think they floated?

Investigate:
Look for Leaves

How many different kinds of leaves can you find?

YOU NEED:
• paper • crayons or markers • glue or tape

Go outside. Look at the leaves on different kinds of plants.

If you find a leaf on the ground, glue or tape it on paper. How can you find out what kind of plant grew the leaf?

Birch

Elm

Oak

Maple

Ash

Fir

TALK ABOUT IT!

• What shapes are the leaves?
• Make the shapes with your hands.
• How are your leaves the same? How are they different?
• Why do you think plants grow leaves?

189

Investigate more: Leaf-Alikes

Match each leaf with a shape that looks like it. Then go outside. Look for leaves that match these leaves, too.

Track a Tree

YOU NEED:
- camera or smart phone
- notebook • glue or tape

Choose a nearby tree. Take a picture of it with a camera or a smart phone. Put the photo in your notebook. Take pictures of it all year. How does your tree look in the fall? What happens in winter?

Needles are thin leaves. They grow on trees such as pines and firs. Can you find a tree with needles?

TALK ABOUT IT!
Why might your tree look different at certain times of the year?

Investigate:
Melt It!

What makes ice melt? Test to find out.

YOU NEED:
- 2 ice cubes
- a cup of cold water
- a cup of warm water

Water can be a liquid. You can pour it into a container. Water can also turn into a solid. Solid water is ice.

1. Use your fingers to feel the water in both cups.
2. Put one ice cube into the warm water.
3. Put the other ice cube into the cold water.
4. Predict what will happen to each ice cube.

TALK ABOUT IT!

- Which ice cube melted first?
- Was your prediction correct?
- What do you think would happen if you put one ice cube in a sunny spot and the other one in the shade?

Investigate more: Freeze It!

Find out whether fresh water or salt water freezes faster.

YOU NEED:
- 2 plastic cups
- 2 tablespoons of salt
- a spoon

1. Fill both plastic cups half full of water.

2. Add 2 tablespoons of salt to one of the cups. Stir until the salt disappears in the water.

3. Put both cups in the freezer.

4. Make a prediction about which cup of water will freeze first.

5. Wait about 2 hours. Then open the freezer and check the cups.

Ice is solid, but it is lighter than liquid water. That's why ice cubes float in a glass of water instead of sinking!

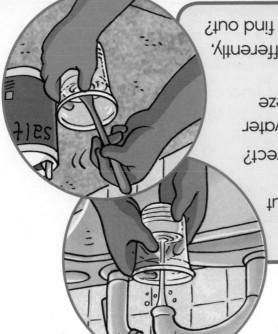

TALK ABOUT IT!

- What do you notice about the two cups of water?
- Was your prediction correct?
- Why do you think fresh water and salt water might freeze differently?
- Do you think they melt differently, too? How can you test to find out?